MATHS Plus

A Book of Mental Mathematics

1

AF883694

GOYAL BROTHERS PRAKASHAN
New Delhi-110055

GOYAL BROTHERS PRAKASHAN
EDUCATIONAL PUBLISHERS

Sales & Registered Office :
11/1903, Chuna Mandi, Paharganj, New Delhi - 110055
Post Box : 5720, Phones : 43551877, 43561877
E-mail : info@goyal-books.com
Website : www.goyal-books.com

Administrative Office :
D-231, Sector 63, Noida-201301 (U.P.)
Phone : 0120-4655555

SHOWROOMS

Ahmedabad : Y-10, Dev Castle Complex Opp. Radhekrishan Villa, Jaymala-Govindwadi Road Isanpur, Ahmedabad–382 443 (Gujarat) Tel : 09925004030

Chennai : No. 50/39, Ground Floor, Five Furlolng Road, Guindy, Chennai-600 032 (Tamil Nadu) Phones : 044-22552776, 044-22552767

Guwahati : Plot No. 1179, KRB Road, Bharalumukh, near Post Office, Railway Gate No. 8, Guwahati-781009 (Assam), Phone : 0361-2735337

Hyderabad : F-7/8/41, First Floor, Agarwal Chambers, 5-9-1121, King Kothi Road, Hyderabad - 500001, Tele-fax : 23211332

Kochi : Fair Heavens, H.No. 52-2783/A, Shine Road, Vyttila Ernakulam - 682019 (Kerala) Phone : 0484-2305288

Kolkata : No. 203, 2nd Floor, Fomra Towers, 84-A, Acharya Jagdish Chandra Bose Road, Kolkata - 700014, Phone : 033-22262683

Bengaluru : 1681/5/4, Ground Floor, 3rd Main Ramamohanapuram, Bengaluru - 560 021, Phone : 080-23320655

Bhopal : Plot No. 203, Zone-II, M.P. Nagar, Bhopal-462 011 (M.P.), Tele-fax : 0755-4271371

Lucknow : B-319, Sector-B, Mahanagar, Opposite P.A.C Main Gate, Lucknow - 226 006, Phone : 0522-2320841

Patna : Ravi Kiran Apartment, Flat No. 2-A, Second floor, Near Water Pumping Station, Pani Tanki Lane, Pirmohani, Patna – 800003

Nagpur : Thakkar Villa House No. 436 Joshiwadi, Sitabuldi, Nagpur - 440012, Phone : 9823655077

To buy our books online log on to www.goyal-books.com

© *Reserved*

Edition : 2025
₹ 160

Disclaimer
Due care and diligence has been taken while writing, editing and printing the book. Neither the author nor the publishers of the book hold any responsibility for any mistakes that may have inadvertently crept in.

Published & Printed by
Roshan Lal Goyal for Goyal Brothers Prakashan, New Delhi

INTRODUCTION

The revised edition of the book **Math Plus — A Book of Mental Mathematics, Book-1 (for Class 1)** is part of the series **Maths Plus — A Book of Mental Mathematics** (Books 1 to 8). This is an innovative series meant for Primary and Middle classes to enhance the mental agility of the learners. This book departs from the traditional approach of teaching Mental Mathematics. In the traditional approach, each assignment was a mix-up of different mathematical concepts. But in this book, each assignment covers up only one concept. Also, the assignments in this book have been prepared keeping in mind the sequence followed by the latest NCERT syllabus. Each assignment in the book covers the chapter/concept taught in the textbook based on the latest NCERT syllabus.

Our approach will help in making the mathematical concepts clear to the learners. It will not only improve the mathematical and calculation skills but also develop quick and logical thinking in the learners.

Salient features of the book are :

- Eye-catching illustrations and a child-friendly layout capture the imagination of child and create an interest in the subject.
- Assignments are prepared keeping in mind the age and level of understanding of the learners.
- Test Papers have been given at the end of each chapter. These Test Papers are meant to check the retention capacity and the level of understanding of the students.
- Ample space has been provided for writing the answers.

We are sure that the book will help in building a strong foundation in mathematics for the children and enable them to face the future in a better way.

Suggestions and criticism for the improvement of the book would be highly appreciated.

— The Publishers

CONTENTS

Shapes and Space

Assignment 1

A. Tick (✓) the object which is outside and cross (X) the object which is inside :

B. Tick (✓) the bigger object and cross (X) the smaller object :

C. Tick (✓) the smallest and cross (X) the biggest :

D. Tick (✓) the biggest tree and cross (X) the smallest tree :

Teacher's Signature : ....   Date : ....

Assignment 2

Shapes and Space

A. Tick (✓) the object which is on the top and cross (✗) the object which is at the bottom :

B. Tick (✓) the object nearer to the boy and cross (✗) the object farther from the boy :

C. Tick (✓) the tree nearest to the bird and cross (✗) the tree farthest from the bird :

Teacher's Signature : ....   Date : ....

Assignment 3

Tick (✓) the object which is on the table and cross (×) the object which is under the table :

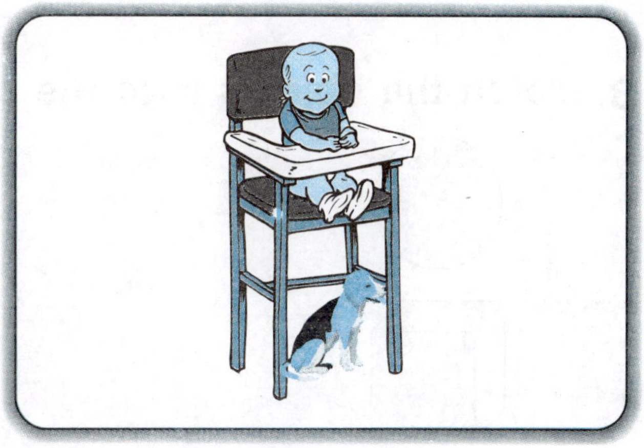

Teacher's Signature : .... Date : ....

Assignment 4

Shapes and Space

A. Tick (✓) the objects that will roll and cross (×) the objects that will slide :

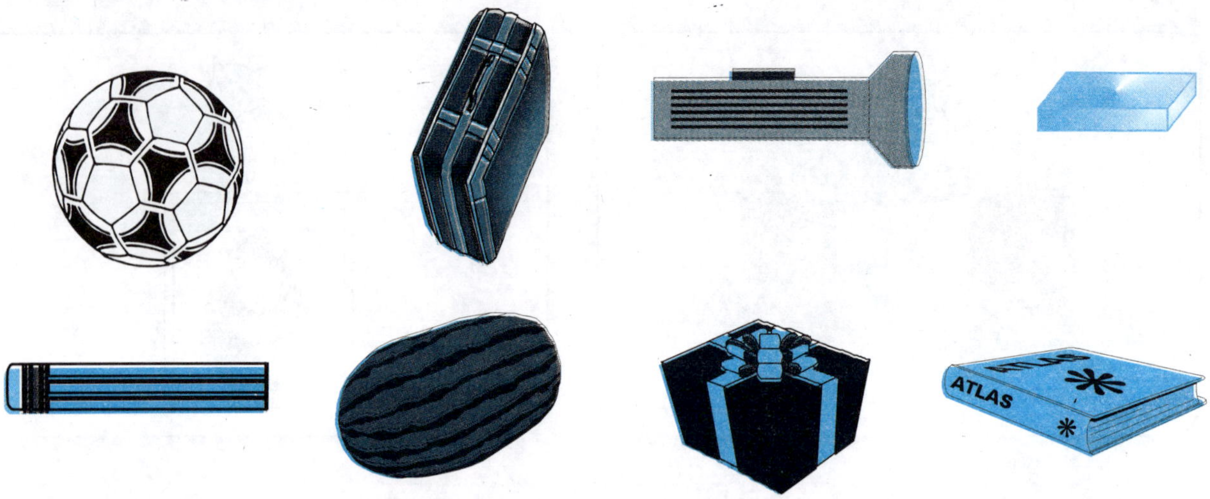

B. Match the objects with the correct shapes :

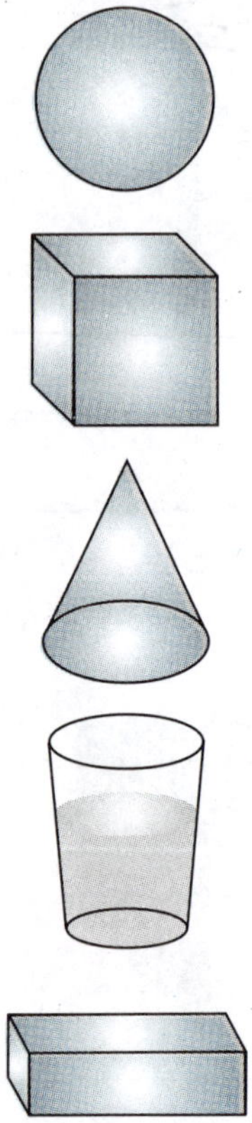

Teacher's Signature : ....   Date : ....

Shapes and Space

Assignment 5

A. Match the shapes of same sizes .

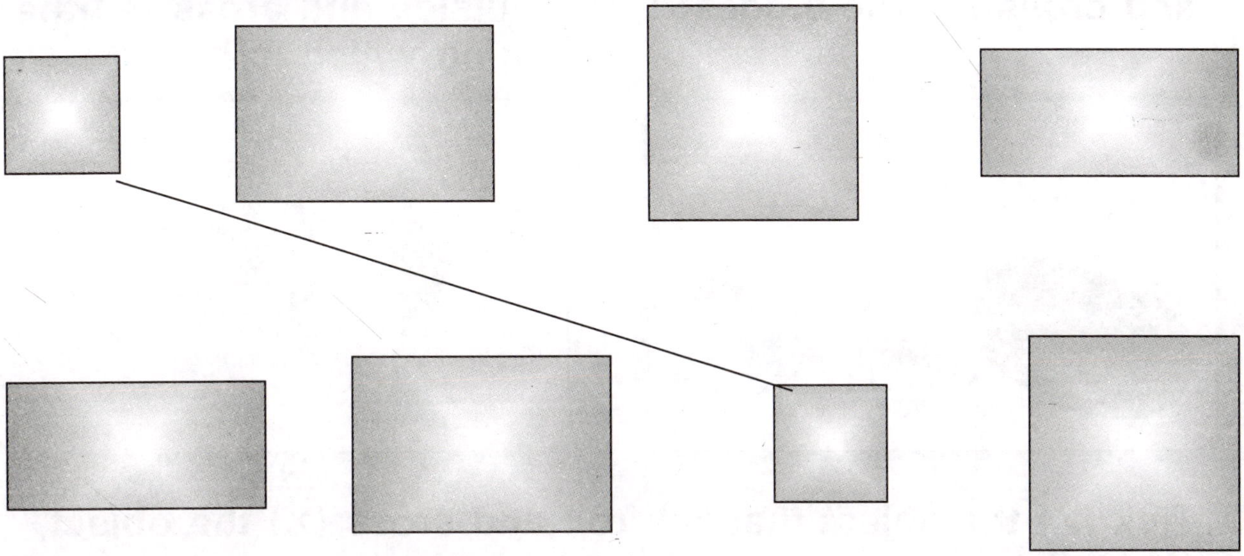

B. Match the same shapes :

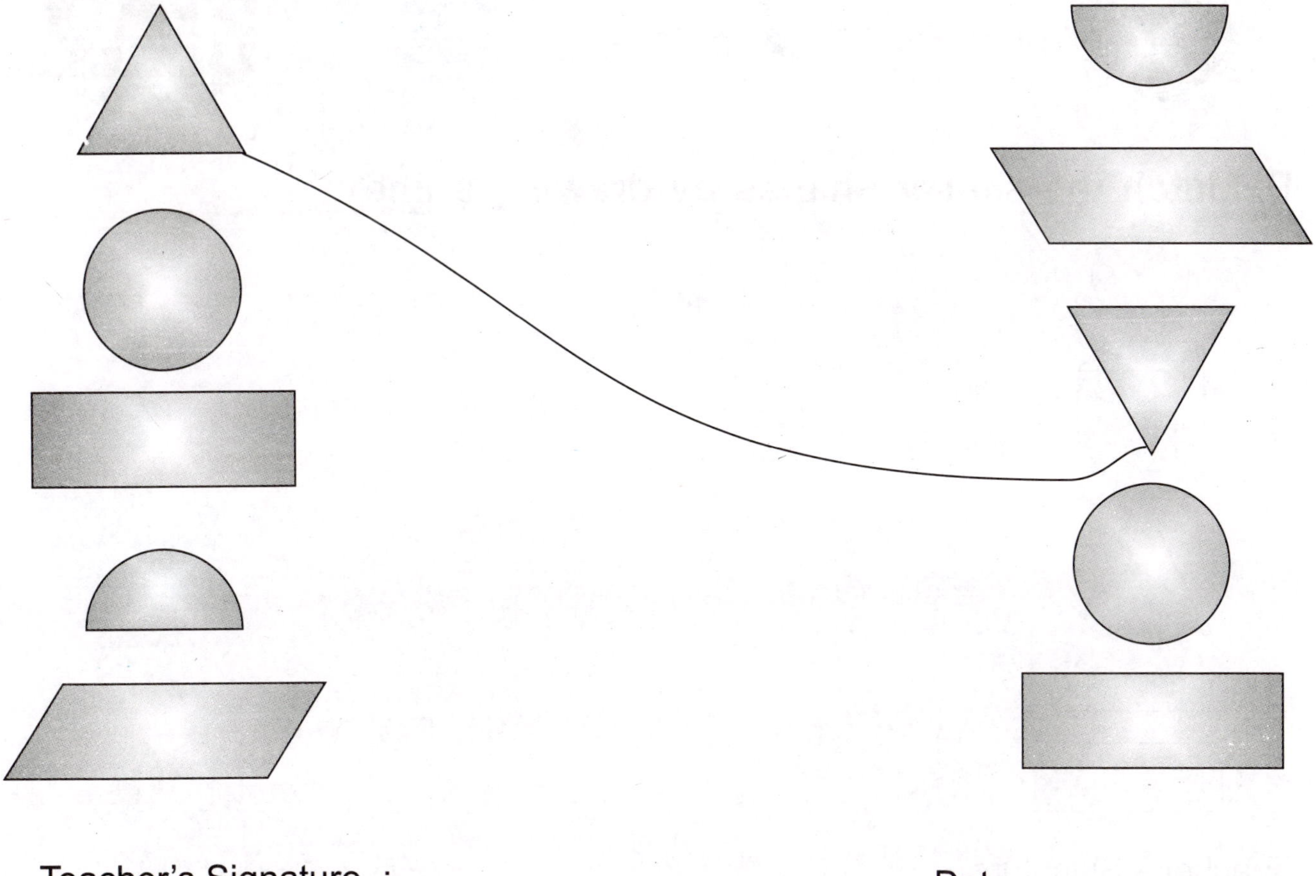

Teacher's Signature : ....

Date : ....

Test 1

A. Tick (✓) the smallest fruit and cross (×) the biggest :

B. Tick (✓) the thing which is outside and cross (×) the thing which is inside :

C. Tick (✓) the object that will roll and cross (×) the object that will slide :

D. Match the similar shapes by drawing a line :

Teacher's Signature : ....   Date : ....

Numbers from One to Nine

Assignment 6

Count and match :

4

3

7

1

9

5

2

6

8

Teacher's Signature : ....

Date : ....

Assignment 7

Numbers from One to Nine

Match the collection with the correct number :

7

5

6

5

8

6

7

8

9

8

6

9

4

6

2

6

4

8

4

8

6

3

8

7

Teacher's Signature : ....   Date : ....

Numbers from One to Nine

Assignment 8

Tick (✓) if both the collections have equal number of objects. Otherwise put a cross (✗) :

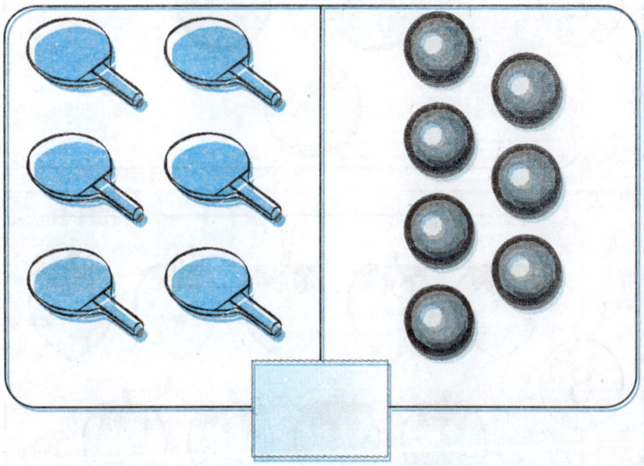

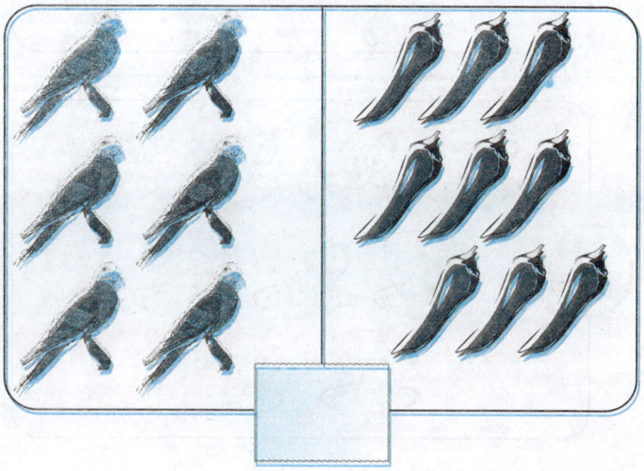

Teacher's Signature : ....

Date : ....

Assignment 9

Numbers from One to Nine

Encircle the objects equal to the number :

4

7

6

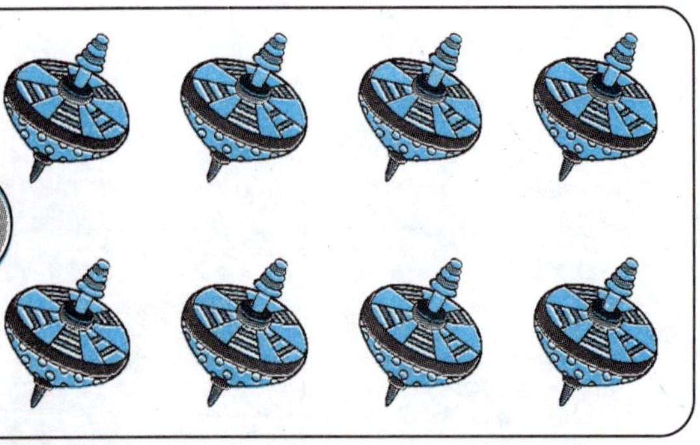

2

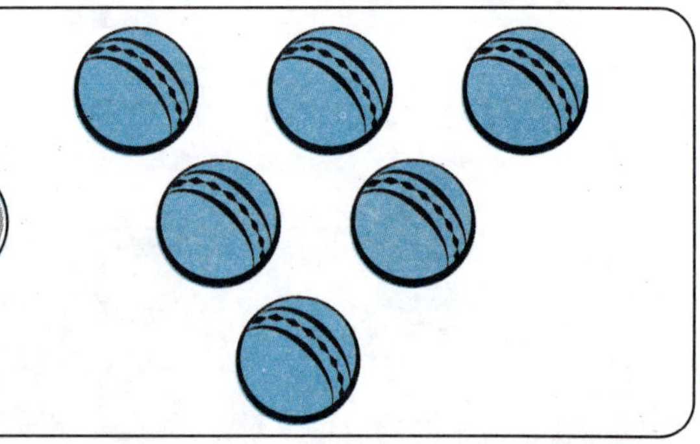

3

8

9

1

Teacher's Signature : ....

Date : ....

Numbers from One to Nine

Assignment 10

Count and encircle the correct number :

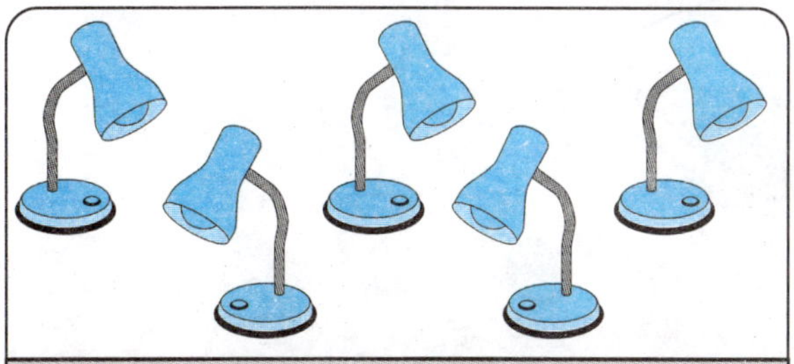

2 5 4

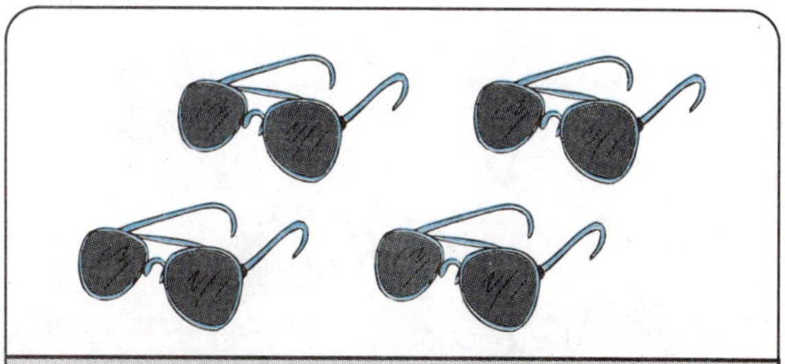

3 5 4

6 7 8

6 4 9

2 4 3

9 8 6

2 3 4

6 9 8

Teacher's Signature : ....

Date : ....

Assignment 11

Numbers from One to Nine

Count and write the number :

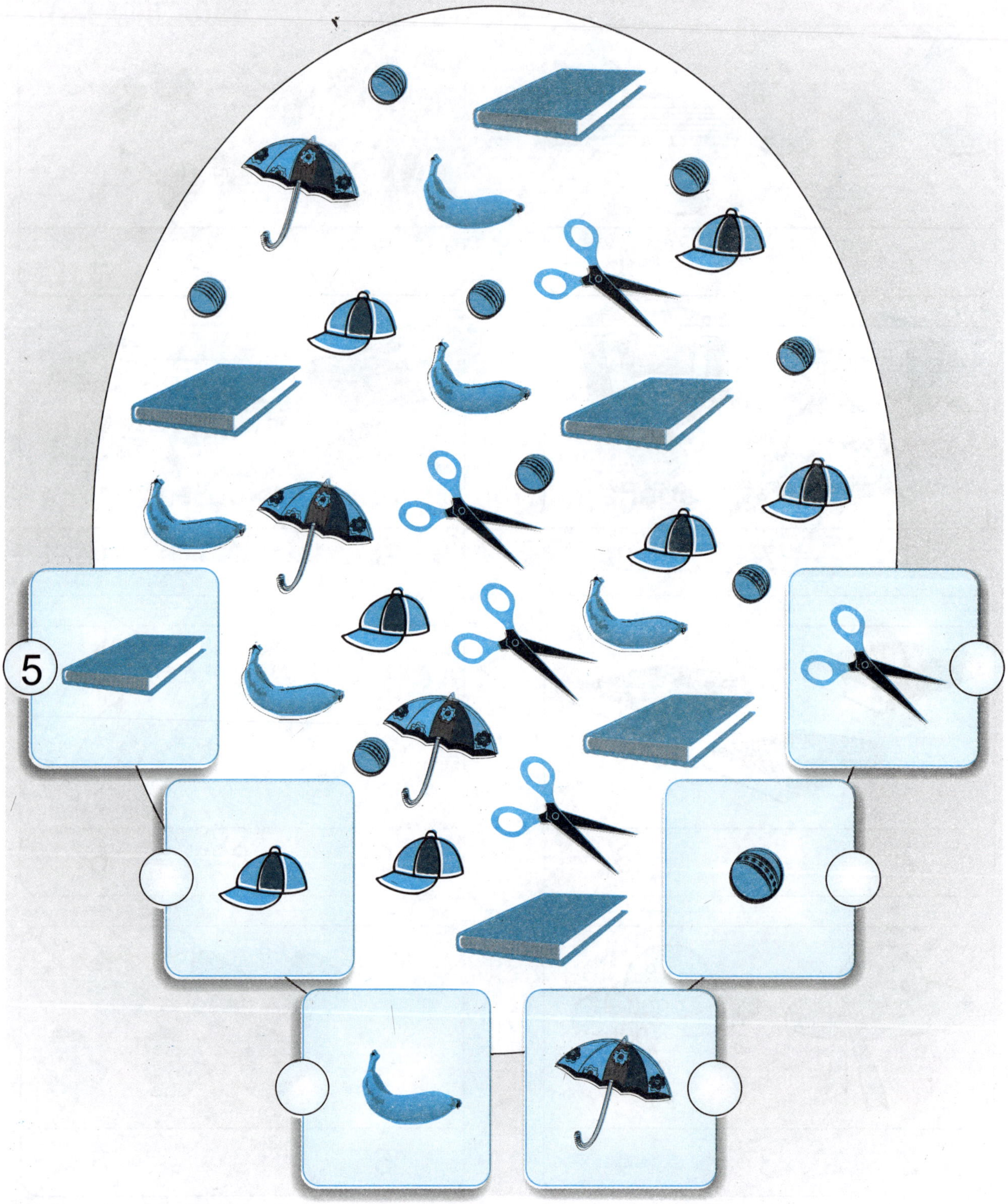

Teacher's Signature : ....

Date : ....

Numbers from One to Nine

Assignment 12

Match the number with the correct collection :

Teacher's Signature : ....

Date : ....

Assignment 13

Numbers from One to Nine

A. Write the number that comes :

Just before

___	3
___	8
___	6
___	5
___	9
___	4

Just after

5	___
7	___
6	___
3	___
8	___
1	___

B. Write the number that comes in between :

6 ___ 8

1 ___ 3

4 ___ 6

7 ___ 9

3 ___ 5

5 ___ 7

2 ___ 4

Teacher's Signature : .... Date : ....

Test 2

A. Write the numbers from 1 to 9 :

1								

B. Count and write :

C. Write the number that comes :

just before		in between			just after	
	5	3		5	7	
	9	6		8	5	

Teacher's Signature : ....

Date : ....

Assignment 14

Addition

Fill in the boxes :

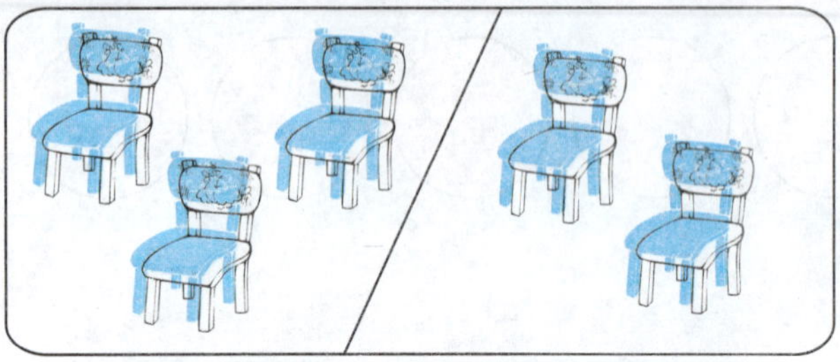

3 and 2 make 5

☐ and ☐ make ☐

☐ and ☐ make ☐

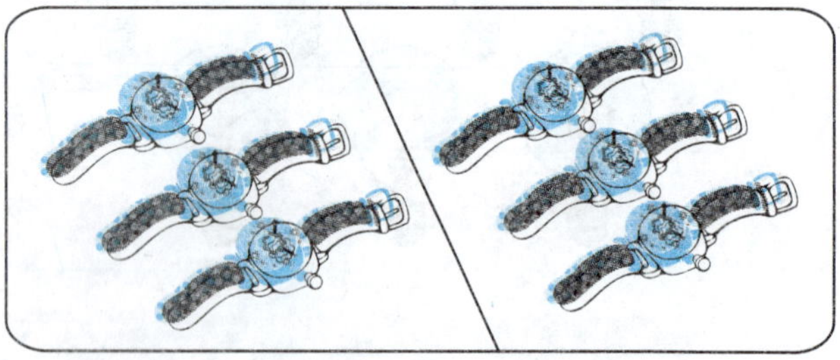

☐ and ☐ make ☐

☐ and ☐ make ☐

☐ and ☐ make ☐

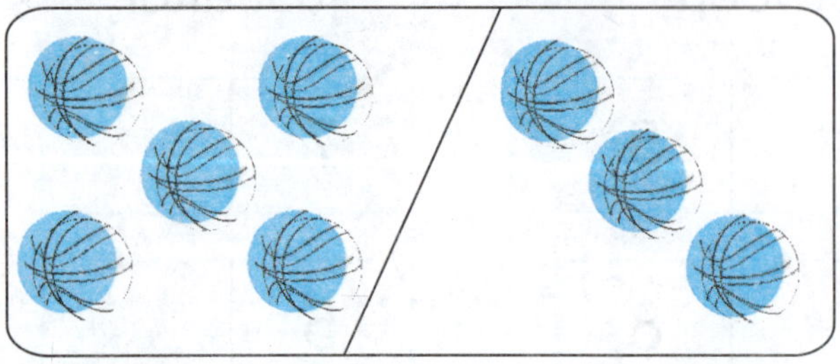

☐ and ☐ make ☐

☐ and ☐ make ☐

Teacher's Signature : ....

Date : ....

Addition

Assignment 15

How many altogether?

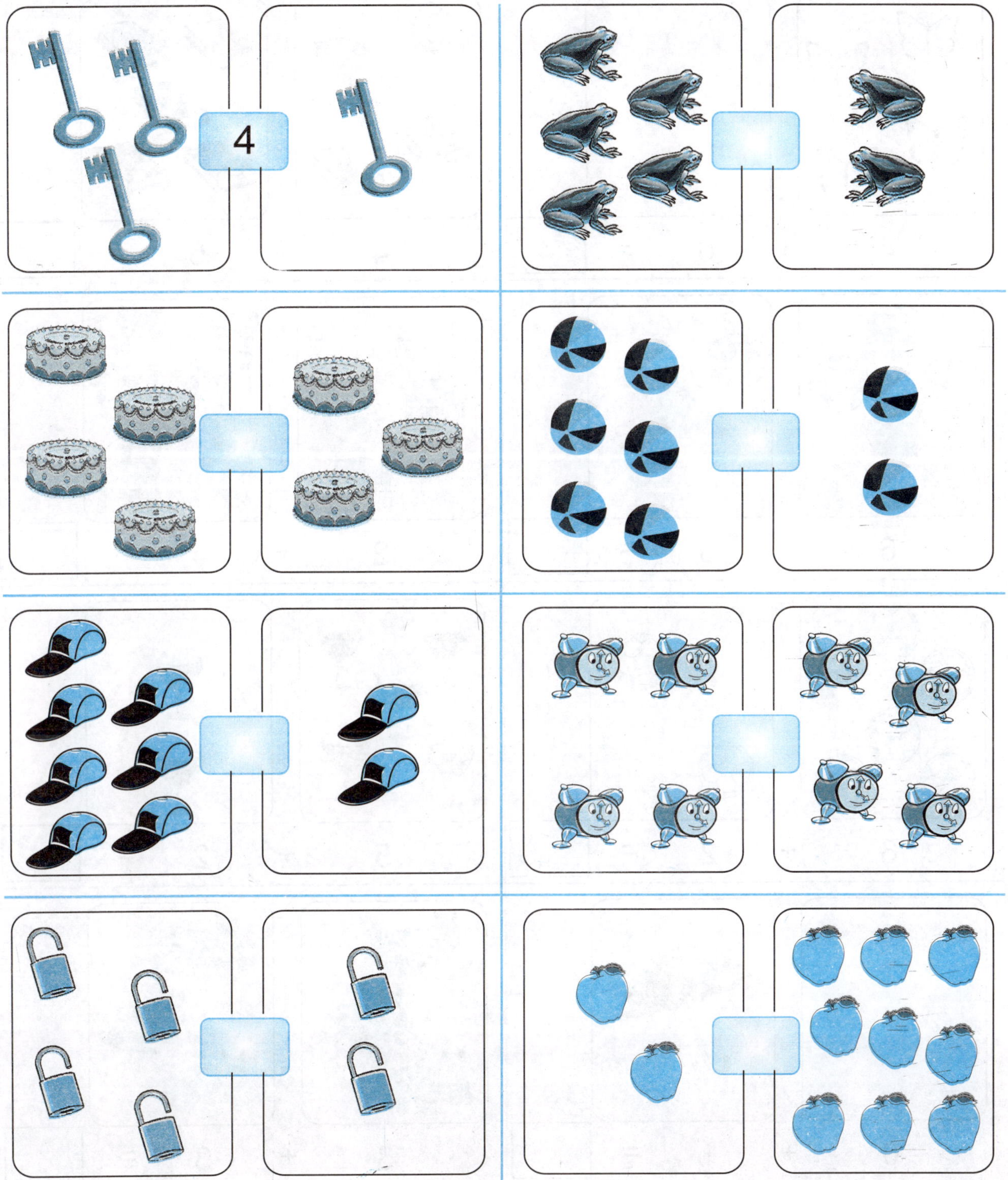

Teacher's Signature : ....

Date : ....

Assignment 16

Addition

Fill in the boxes :

4 + 0 = 4

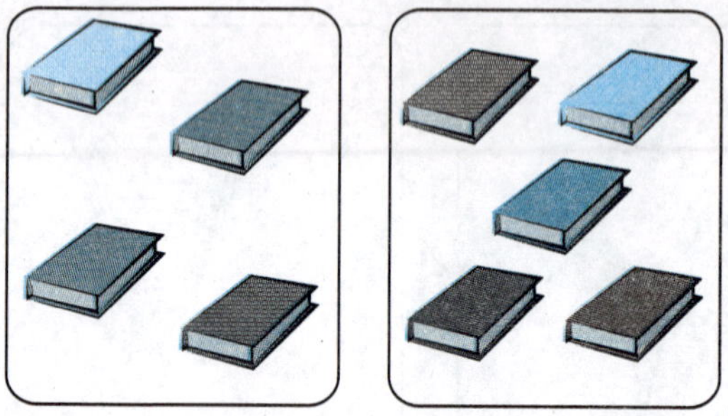

4 + 5 =

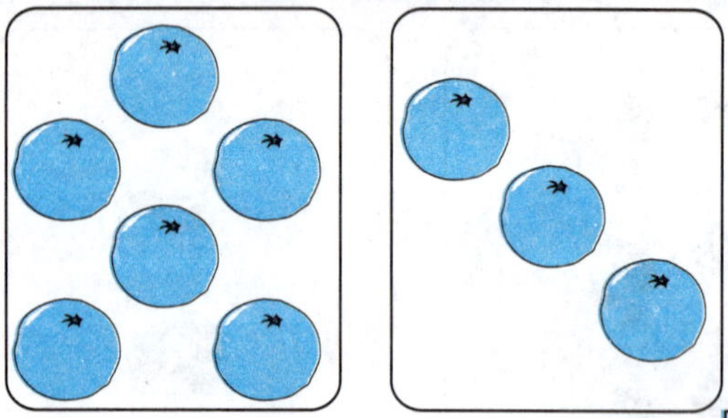

6 + 3 =

2 + 4 =

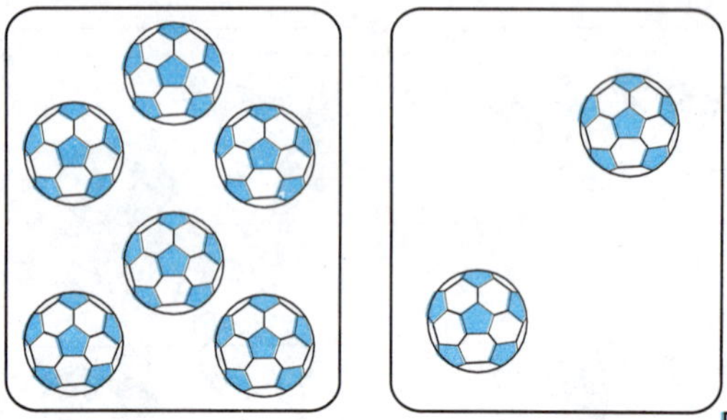

6 + 2 =

5 + 2 =

0 + 1 =

3 + 3 =

Teacher's Signature : ....

Date : ....

Addition

Assignment 17

Fill in the boxes :

3 + 4 = ☐	3 + 2 = ☐
5 + 0 = ☐	5 + 4 = ☐
6 + 3 = ☐	0 + 3 = ☐
2 + 7 = ☐	7 + 1 = ☐

4 + 4 = ☐	5 + 2 = ☐	6 + 3 = ☐	8 + 0 = ☐
3 + 5 = ☐	1 + 5 = ☐	2 + 4 = ☐	2 + 3 = ☐
5 + 0 = ☐	1 + 7 = ☐	8 + 2 = ☐	4 + 3 = ☐

Teacher's Signature : ....

Date : ....

Test 3

Fill in the boxes :

2 + 3 = 5

☐ + ☐ = ☐

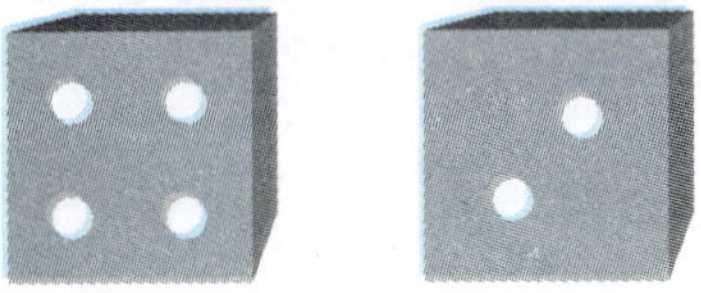

☐ + ☐ = ☐

☐ + ☐ = ☐

☐ + ☐ = ☐

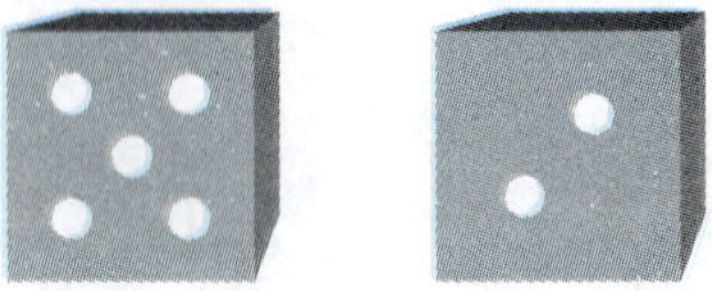

☐ + ☐ = ☐

☐ + ☐ = ☐

☐ + ☐ = ☐

☐ + ☐ = ☐

☐ + ☐ = ☐

Teacher's Signature : ....

Date : ....

Assignment 18

Fill in the boxes :

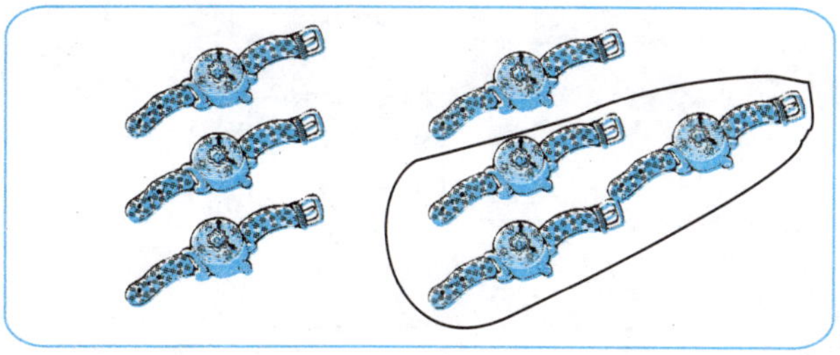

7 take away 3 left 4

9 take away 4 left

5 take away 5 left

8 take away 5 left

9 take away 2 left

6 take away 2 left

9 take away 7 left

7 take away 5 left

Teacher's Signature : ....

Date : ....

Assignment 19

Count and subtract :

5 − 2 =

− =

− =

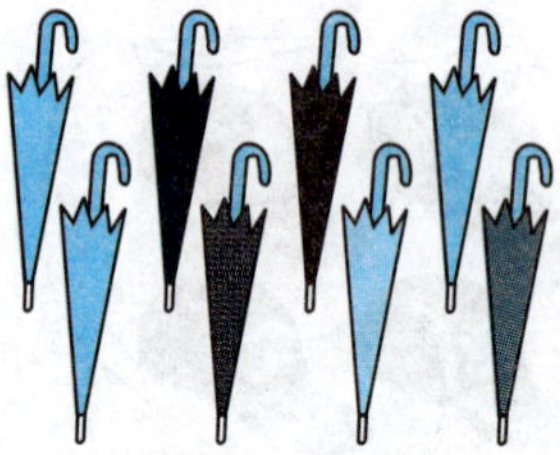  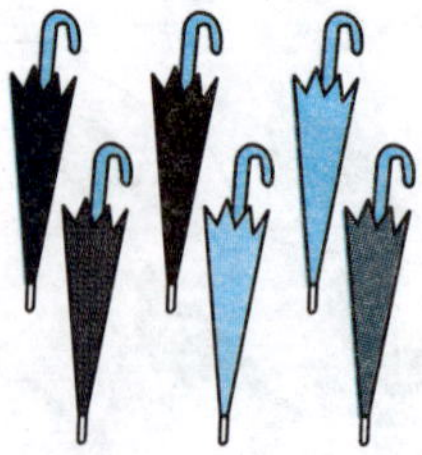

− =

Teacher's Signature : ....   Date : ....

Subtraction

Assignment 20

Subtract :

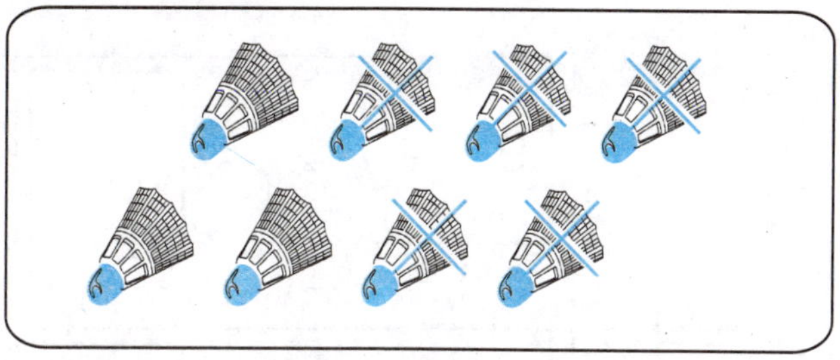

8 — 5 = 3

___ — ___ = ___

___ — ___ = ___

___ — ___ = ___

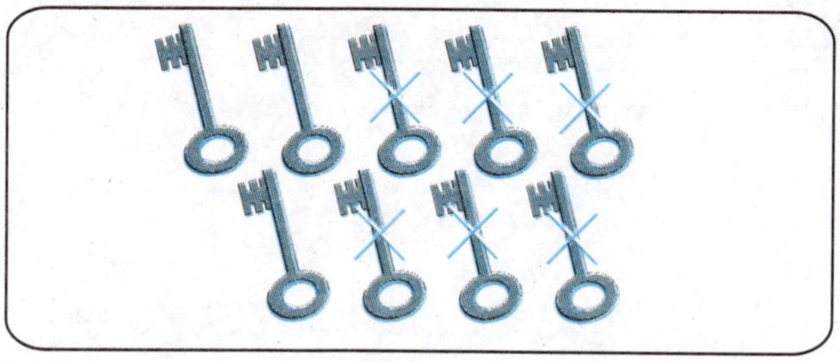

___ — ___ = ___

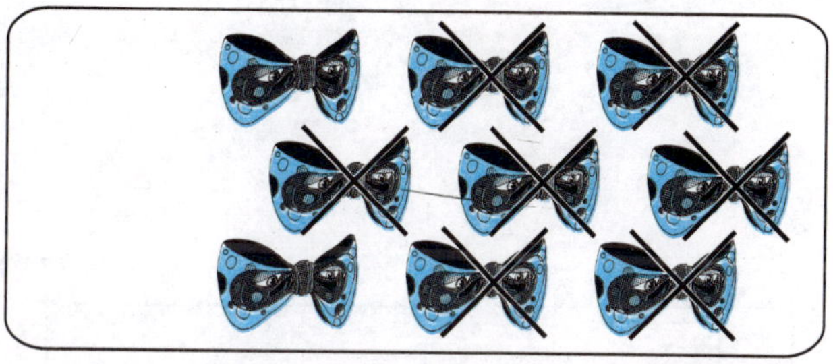

___ — ___ = ___

___ — ___ = ___

___ — ___ = ___

Teacher's Signature : ....

Date : ....

Assignment 21

Fill in the boxes :

5 − 2 = ☐   8 − 7 = ☐   9 − 4 = ☐

5 − 1 = ☐   3 − 3 = ☐   7 − 2 = ☐

8	5	9	7	9
− 3	− 2	− 4	− 1	− 2
☐	☐	☐	☐	☐

6	7	5	6	5
− 5	− 3	− 5	− 4	− 4
☐	☐	☐	☐	☐

☐ − 4 = 2   ☐ − 3 = ☐

8 − ☐ = 5   5 − ☐ = 0

9 − ☐ = 3   ☐ − 7 = 0

Teacher's Signature : ....   Date : ....

Test 4

Join each subtraction sum with the correct answer :

6 – 2	3
6 – 3	1
5 – 5	2
8 – 7	6
6 – 0	8
7 – 5	0
8 – 3	4
9 – 1	5

Teacher's Signature : .... Date : ....

Assignment 22

Numbers from Ten to Twenty

Make a group of 10 and write the numbers :

Ten	Ones
1	2

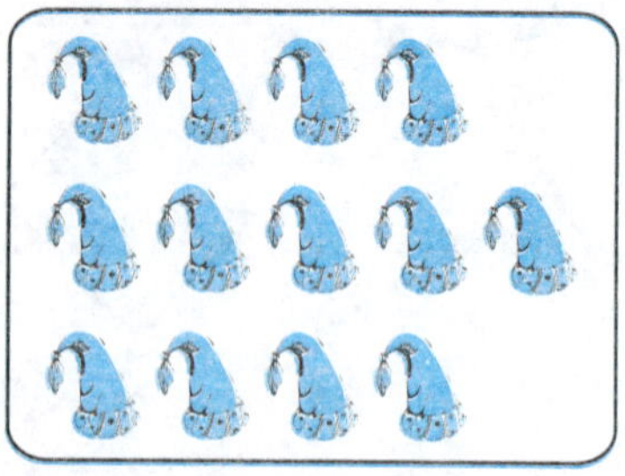

Ten	Ones

Ten	Ones

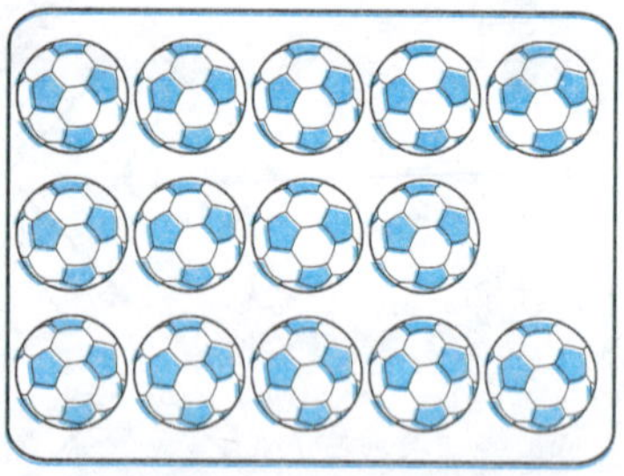

Ten	Ones

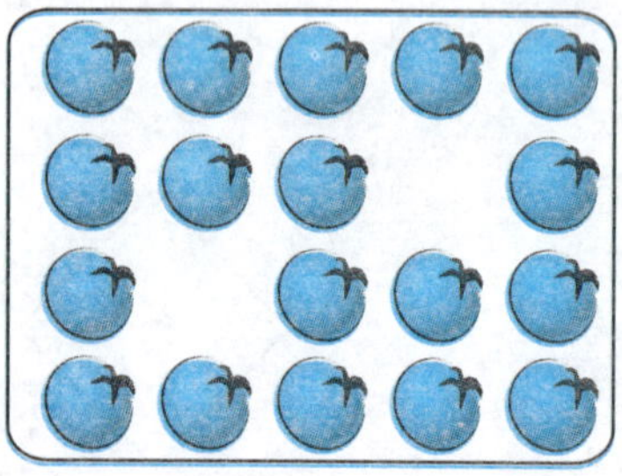

Ten	Ones

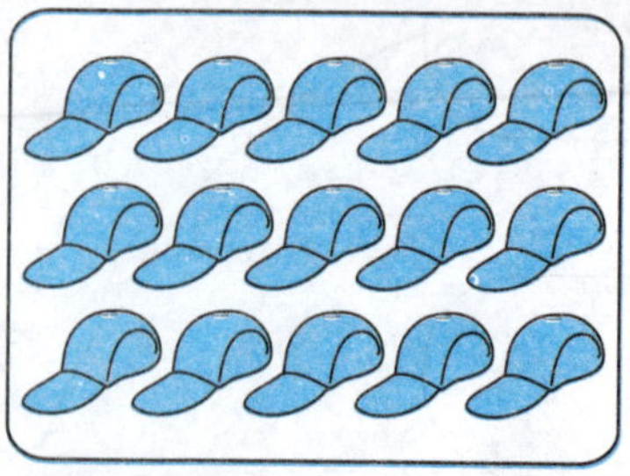

Ten	Ones

Ten	Ones

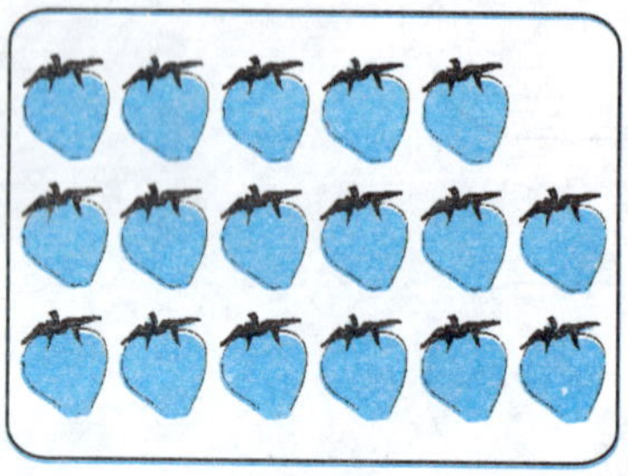

Ten	Ones

Ten	Ones

Ten	Ones

Teacher's Signature : ....

Date : ....

Numbers from Ten to Twenty

Assignment 23

A. Fill in the numbers from 1 to 20 :

1				5			8		10
	12					17			20

B. Fill in the numbers from 20 to 1 :

20						14			11
10				6			3		

C. Write the missing numbers :

10	11					16

14	15					20

12	13					18

11	12					17

Teacher's Signature : ....   Date : ....

Assignment 24

Numbers from Ten to Twenty

A. Fill in the missing numbers :

13			16				20
		12		14			17

B. Write the number that comes just after :

16		18	
14		11	

C. Write the number that comes just before :

	18		15
	13		17

D. Write the number that comes in between :

14		16	15		17	11		13
10		12	13		15	18		20

E. Circle the biggest number :

12	15	6	13	16	19

F. Circle the smallest number :

14	16	12	15	7	20

Teacher's Signature : ....

Date : ....

Numbers from Ten to Twenty

Assignment 25

A. Add :

8 + 7 = ☐	13 + 5 = ☐	6 + 7 = ☐
9 + 9 = ☐	12 + 7 = ☐	14 + 5 = ☐

5	6	15	13	6
+ 7	+ 8	+ 3	+ 5	+ 9
☐	☐	☐	☐	☐

B. Subtract :

18 – 5 = ☐	15 – 6 = ☐	12 – 4 = ☐
13 – 0 = ☐	17 – 6 = ☐	19 – 8 = ☐

17	15	19	17	13
– 6	– 4	– 5	– 2	– 5
☐	☐	☐	☐	☐

Teacher's Signature : .... Date : ....

Test 5

A. Fill in the boxes :

1 ten 2 ones = ☐	☐ ten 6 ones = 16
1 ten 5 ones = ☐	☐ ten 1 one = 11
1 ten 9 ones = ☐	1 ten ☐ ones = 18
1 ten 7 ones = ☐	1 ten ☐ ones = 13

B. Circle the biggest number and cross the smallest number :

8	5	7	3	15	11	14	15	18
9	12	16	8	2	17	19	16	17
5	13	16	15	19	9	14	11	13

C. Fill in the boxes :

☐ + 7 = 13	11 − ☐ = 8	11 + 3 = ☐
4 + ☐ = 11	☐ + 9 = 14	15 − ☐ = 4
6 − ☐ = 0	8 − ☐ = 8	☐ + 14 = 14

Teacher's Signature : ....   Date : ....

Time

Assignment 26

A. Number the activities in sequence.

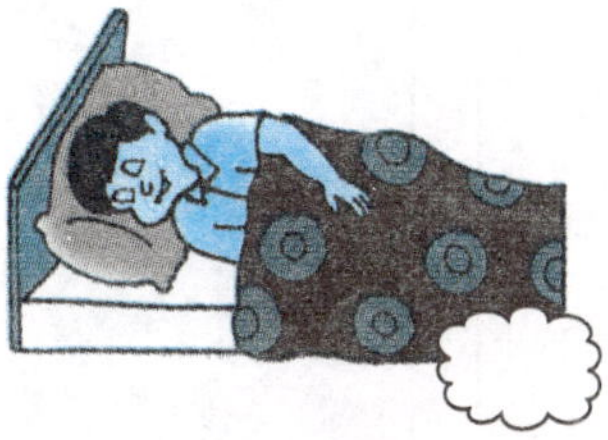

B. Write T for true statements and F for false statements :

We take breakfast in the afternoon.	
We take dinner in the night.	
We play in the evening.	
We go to sleep in the morning.	
We take bath in the morning.	

Teacher's Signature : ....

Date : ....

Assignment 27

Measurement

Tick (✓) the longer and cross (✗) the shorter :

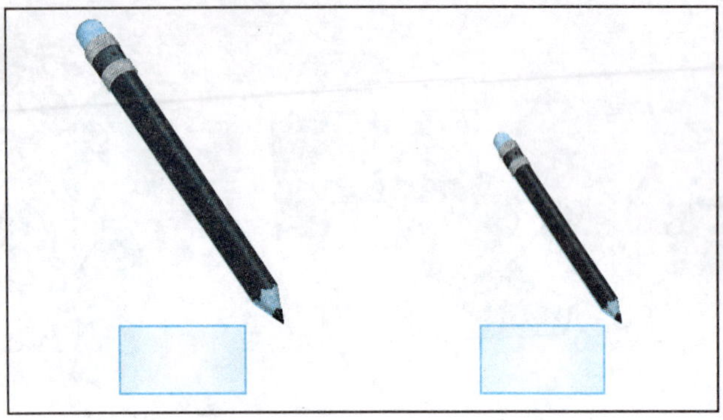
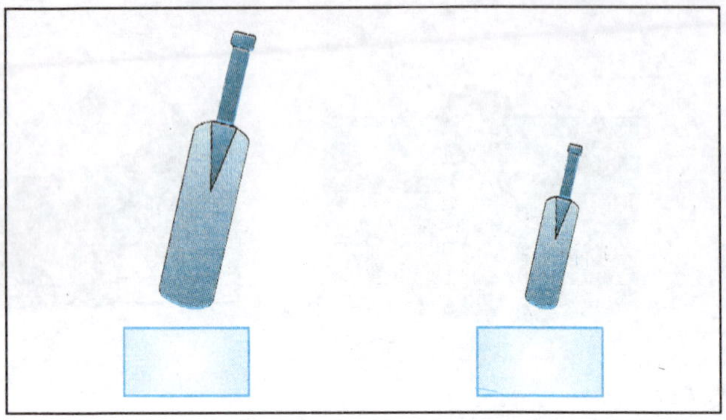
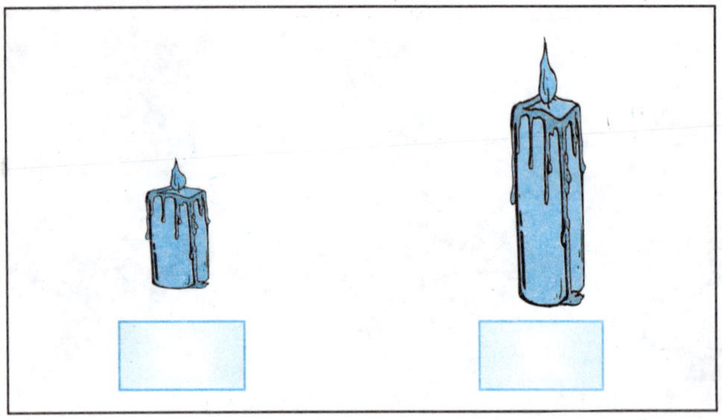
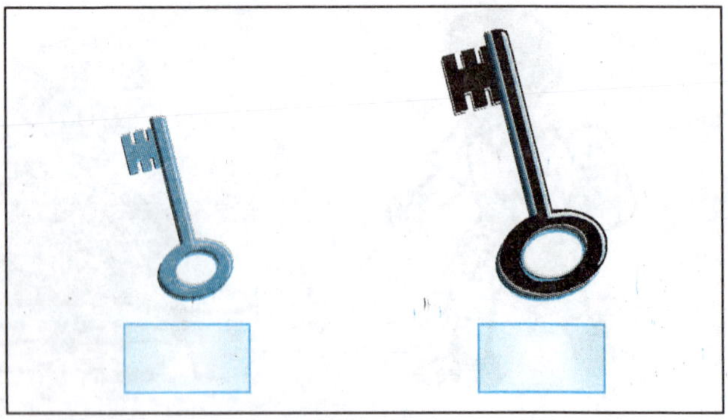
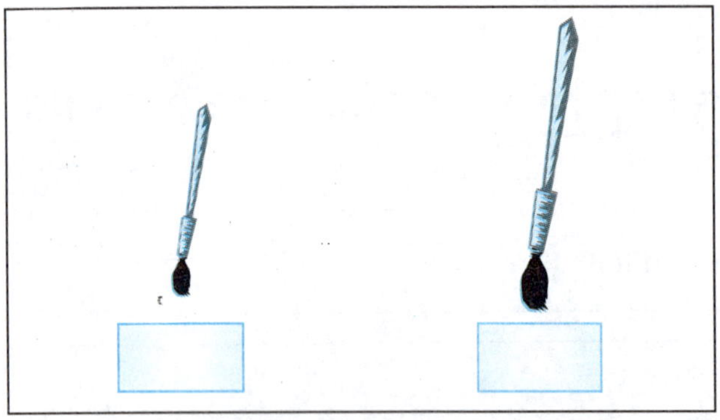
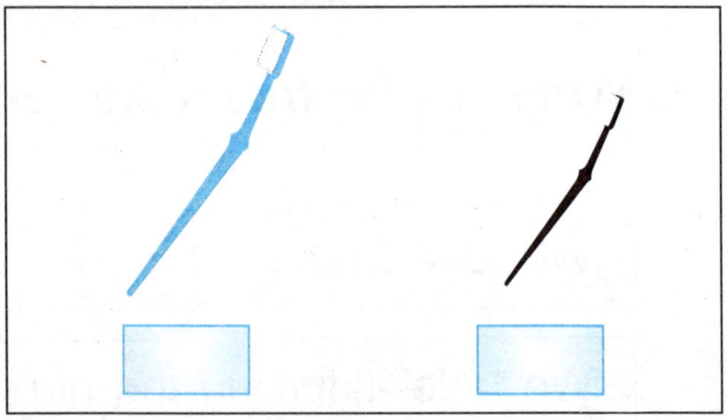
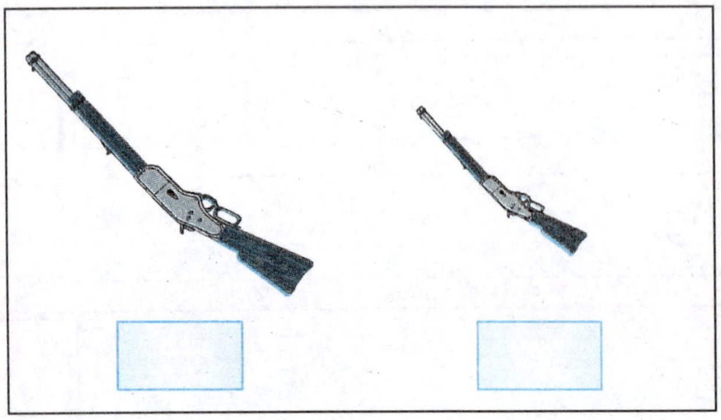
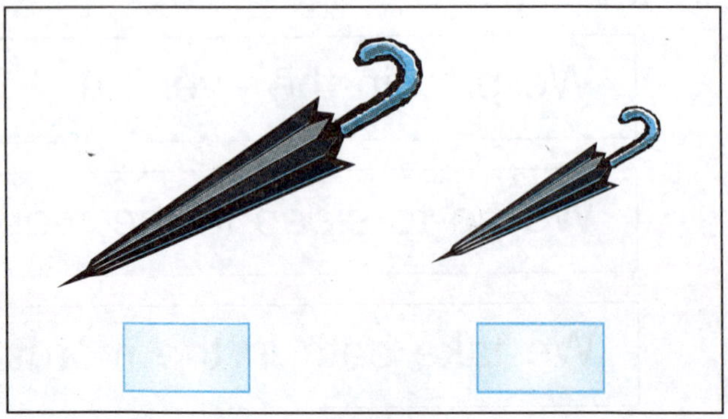

Teacher's Signature : .... Date : ....

Measurement

Assignment 28

Tick (✓) the longest and cross (✗) the shortest :

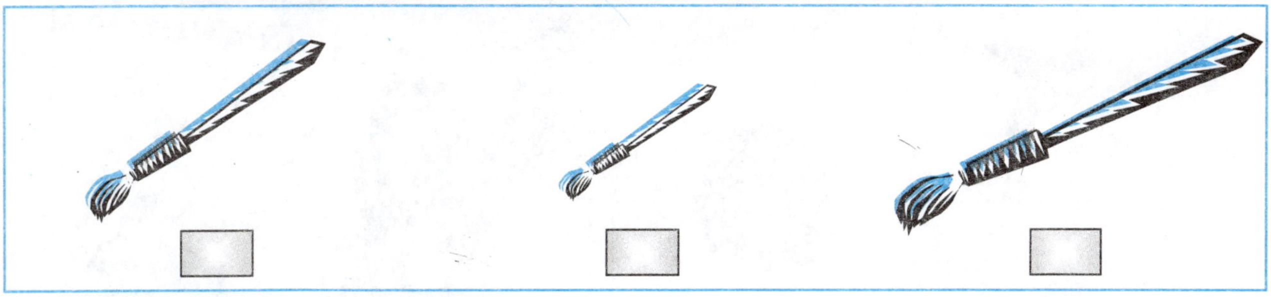

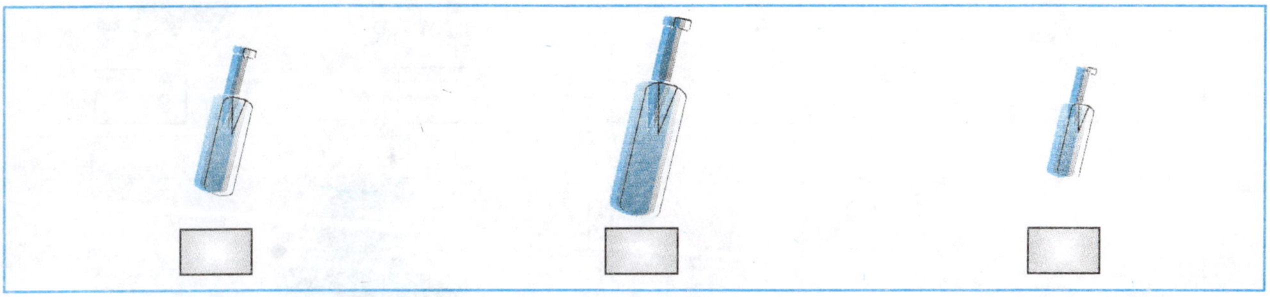

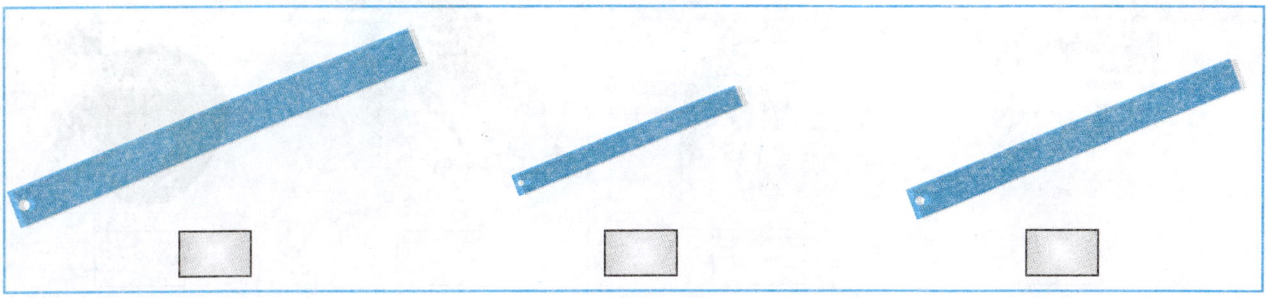

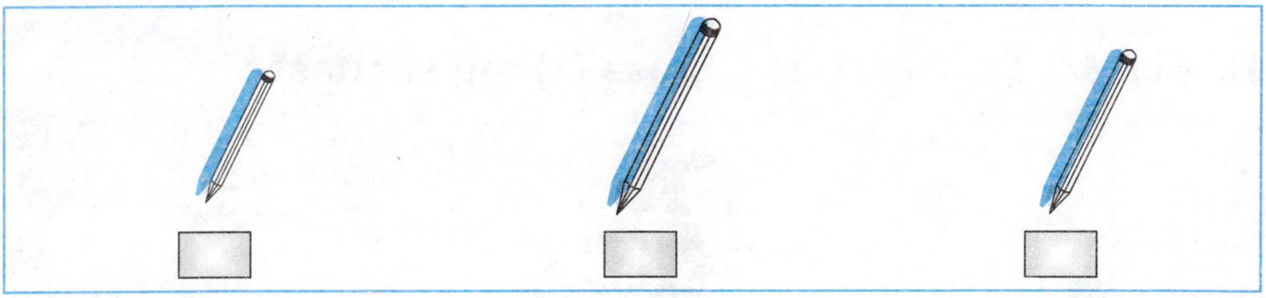

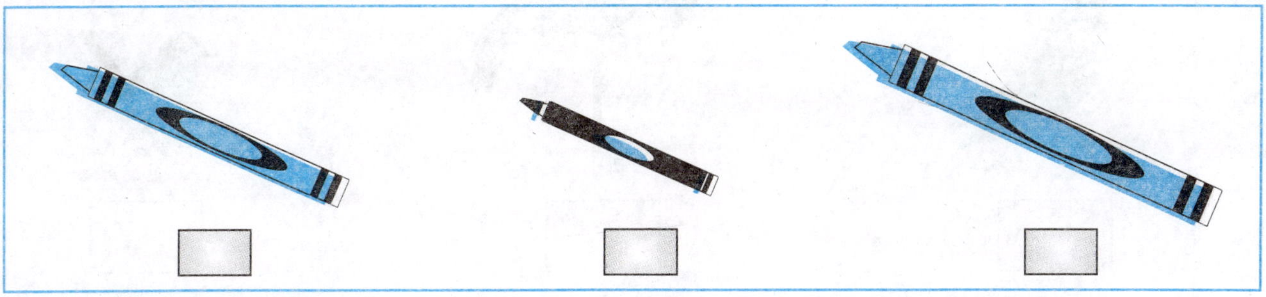

Teacher's Signature : ....

Date : ....

Assignment 29

A. Tick (✓) the taller and cross (✗) the shorter :

B. Tick (✓) the tallest and cross (✗) the shortest :

Teacher's Signature : ....

Date : ....

Measurement **Assignment 30**

A. Tick (✓) the thicker and cross (✗) the thinner :

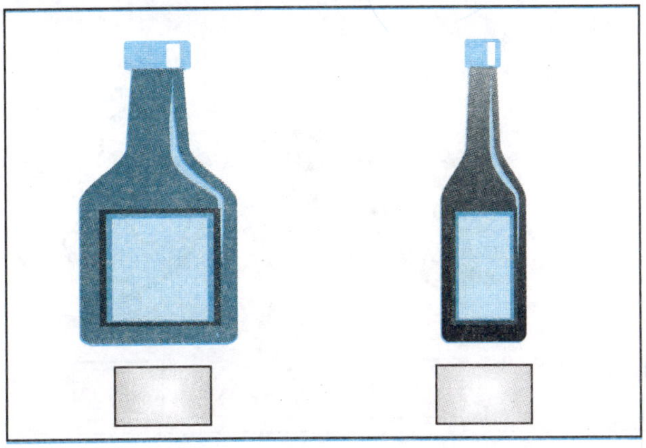

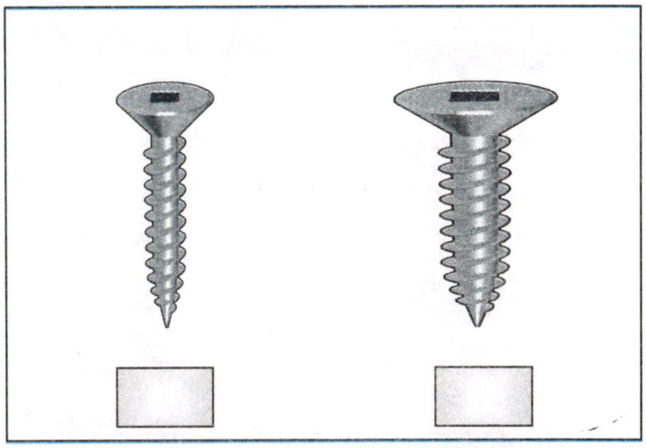

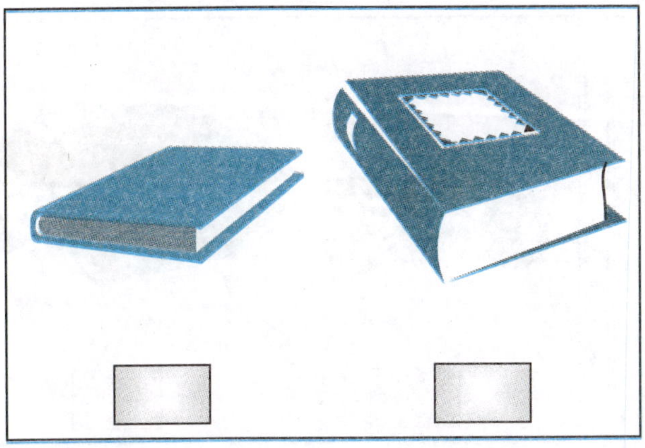

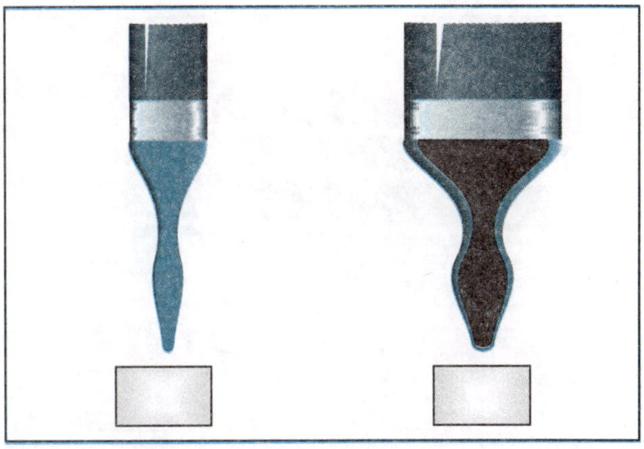

B. Tick (✓) the thickest and cross (✗) the thinnest :

Teacher's Signature : .... Date : ....

Assignment 31

A. Tick (✓) the heavier and cross (✗) the lighter :

B. Tick (✓) the heaviest and cross (✗) the lightest :

Teacher's Signature : ....

Date : ....

Test 6

A. Tick (✓) the activities that you do in the morning and cross (✕) the activities that you do in the night :

B. Tick (✓) the tallest and cross (✗) the shortest :

C. Tick (✓) the longest and cross (✗) the shortest :

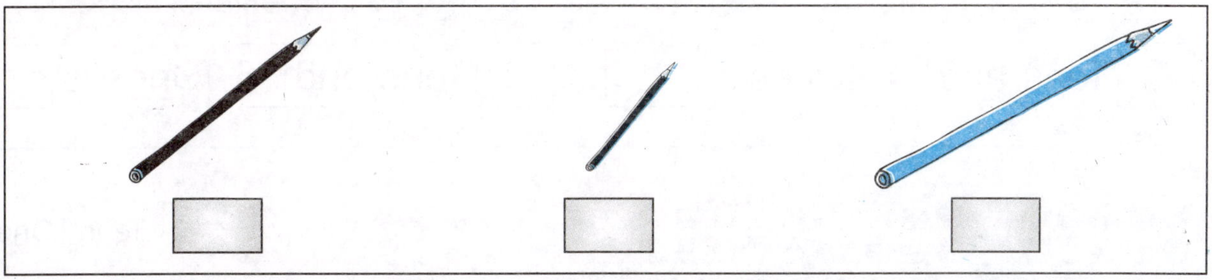

D. Tick (✓) the thickest and cross (✗) the thinnest :

Teacher's Signature : ....

Date : ....

Assignment 32   Numbers from Twenty-one to Fifty

Fill in the boxes :

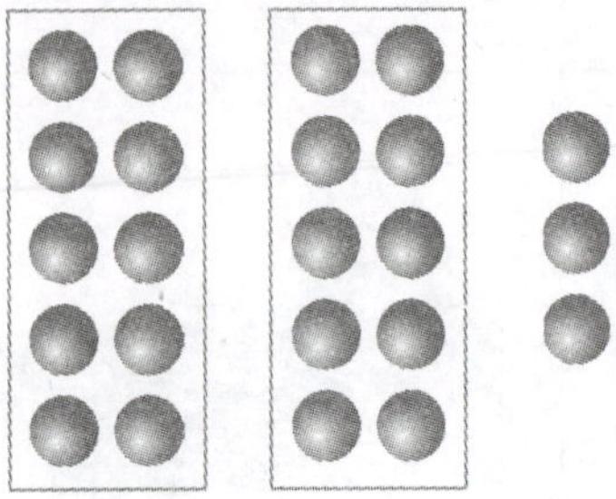

Tens	Ones
2	3

2 Tens and 3 Ones is 23

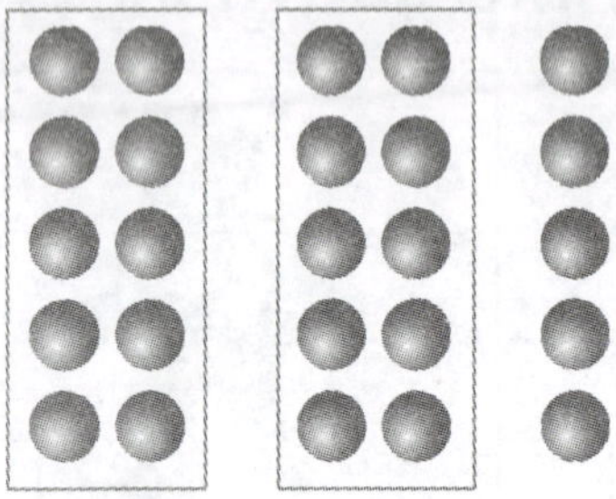

Tens	Ones

2 Tens and 5 Ones is ____

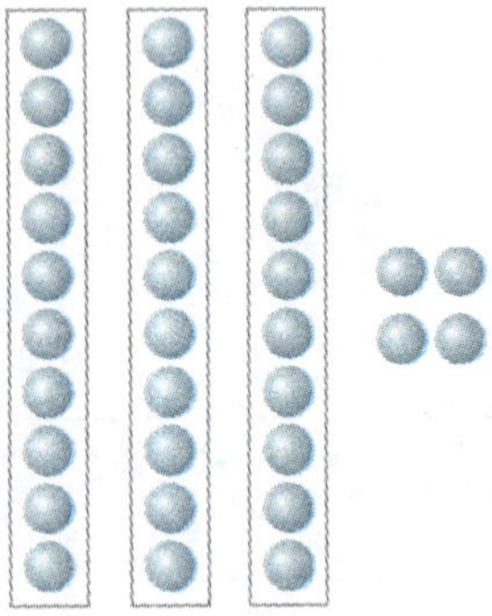

Tens	Ones

3 Tens and 4 Ones is ____

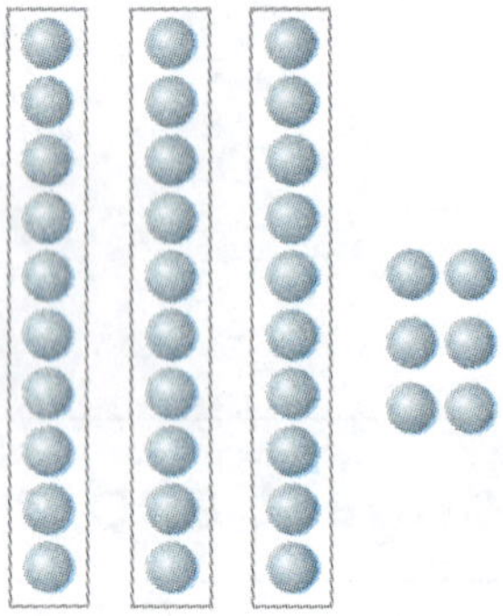

Tens	Ones

3 Tens and 6 Ones is ____

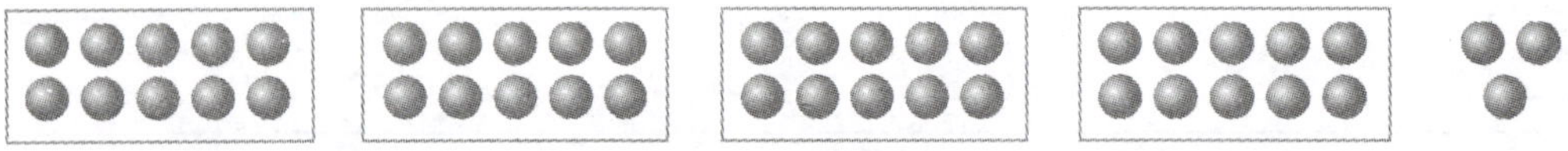

Tens	Ones

4 Tens and 3 Ones is ____

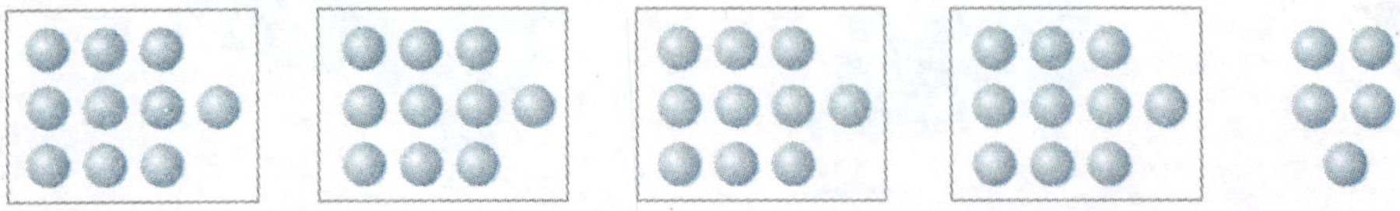

Tens	Ones

4 Tens and 5 Ones is ____

Teacher's Signature : ....

Date : ....

Numbers from Twenty-one to Fifty

Assignment 33

A. Fill up the missing numbers :

1					6				10
11			14						20
						27			
31							38		
	42			45					50

B. Write as tens and ones :

24 is ☐ tens ☐ ones

28 is ☐ tens ☐ ones

26 is ☐ tens ☐ ones

31 is ☐ tens ☐ one

35 is ☐ tens ☐ ones

40 is ☐ tens ☐ ones

47 is ☐ tens ☐ ones

49 is ☐ tens ☐ ones

Teacher's Signature : ....

Date : ....

Test 7

A. Write as tens and ones :

21 is [ ] tens [ ] one

25 is [ ] tens [ ] ones

44 is [ ] tens [ ] ones

46 is [ ] tens [ ] ones

39 is [ ] tens [ ] ones

B. Tick (✓) 'YES' or 'NO' :

40 and 3 make 43	YES	NO	30 and 9 make 39	YES	NO
30 and 7 make 38	YES	NO	40 and 6 make 36	YES	NO
40 and 5 make 5	YES	NO	20 and 8 make 28	YES	NO

C. Fill up the missing numbers :

21					26	27	

35	36						42

28	29						35

Teacher's Signature : ....   Date : ....

Assignment 34

Count the number of letters in each name :

Names	Number of letters
A M I T →	
S A R I K A →	
A J A Y →	
J O H N →	
S O H A I L →	
R A V I →	
G E E T A →	
A M I T A B H →	

How many names have four letters? ☐

How many names have six letters? ☐

How many names have seven letters? ☐

How many names starts from letter A? ☐

How many names starts from letter S? ☐

Teacher's Signature : .... Date : ....

Assignment 35

A. Extend the sequence :

B. What comes next in the sequence?

Teacher's Signature : ....

Date : ....

Patterns

Assignment 36

A. Fill in the boxes in sequence :

B. Study the pattern and fill in the missing numbers :

C. Complete the pattern.

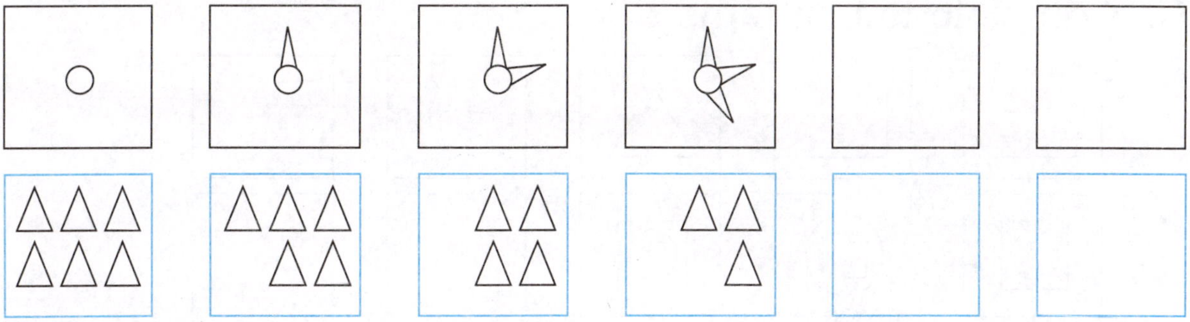

Teacher's Signature : ....

Date : ....

Test 8

A. Observe the picture and fill in the boxes :

How many  are there ? ☐

How many  are there ? ☐

How many  are there ? ☐

How many  are there ? ☐

How many  are there ? ☐

How many  are there ? ☐

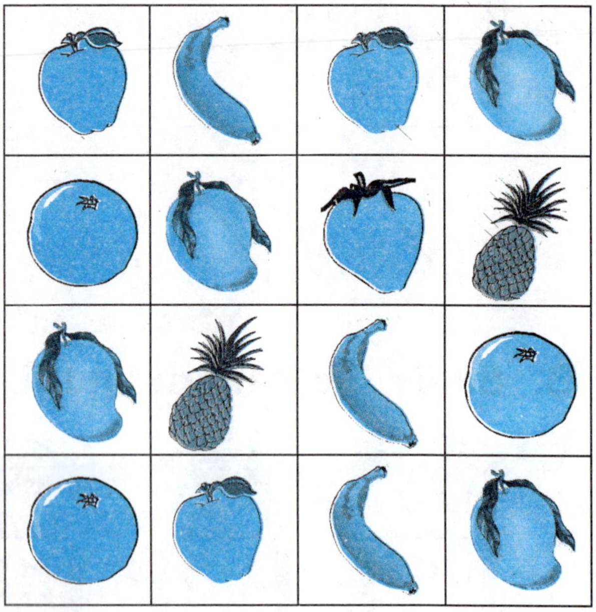

B. Study the pattern and fill in the missing numbers :

3 — 8 — 13 — ☐ — ☐ — ☐

7 — 10 — 13 — ☐ — ☐ — ☐

5 ~ 15 ~ 25 ~ △ ~ △ ~ △

C. Complete the patterns :

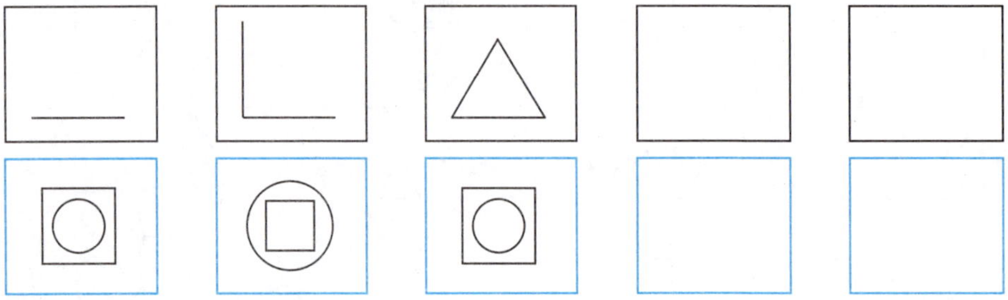

Teacher's Signature : .... Date : ....

Assignment 37

Write the number :

Tens	Ones

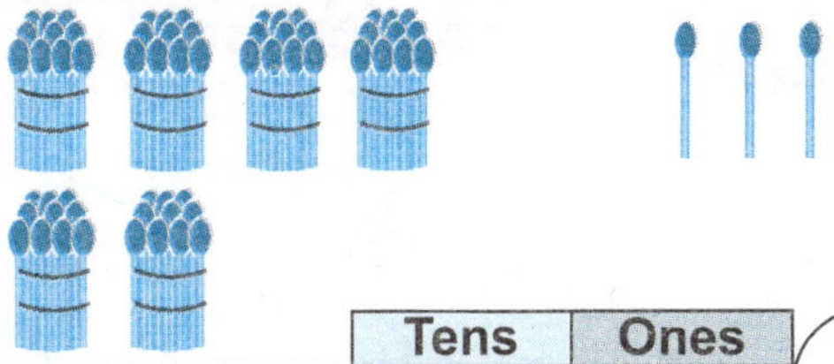

Tens	Ones

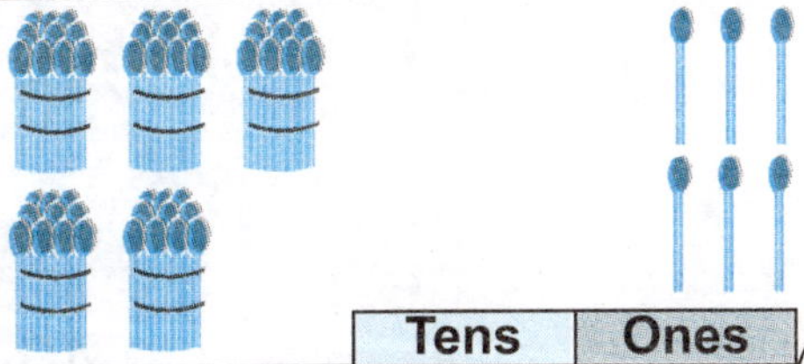

Tens	Ones

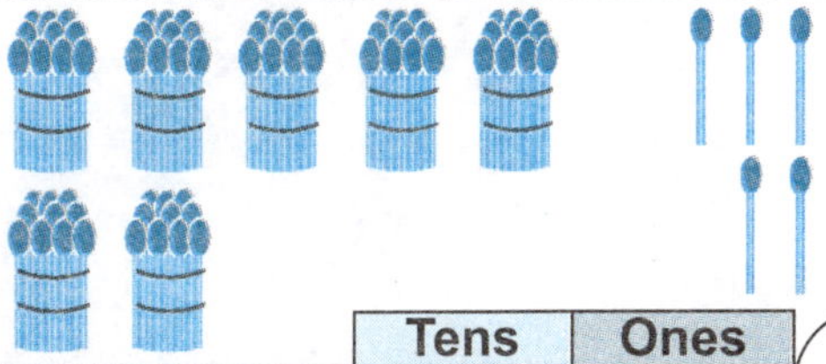

Tens	Ones

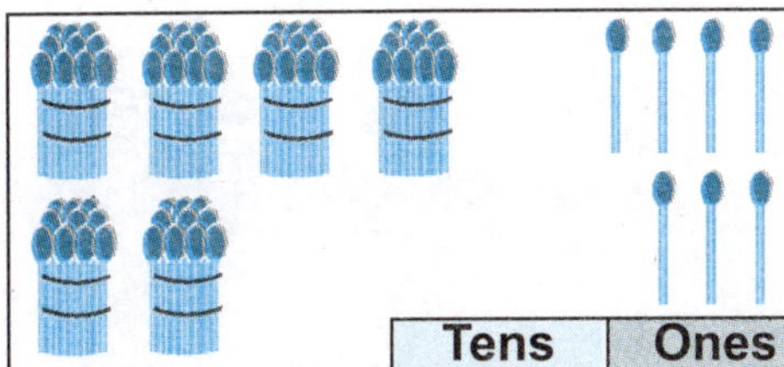

Tens	Ones

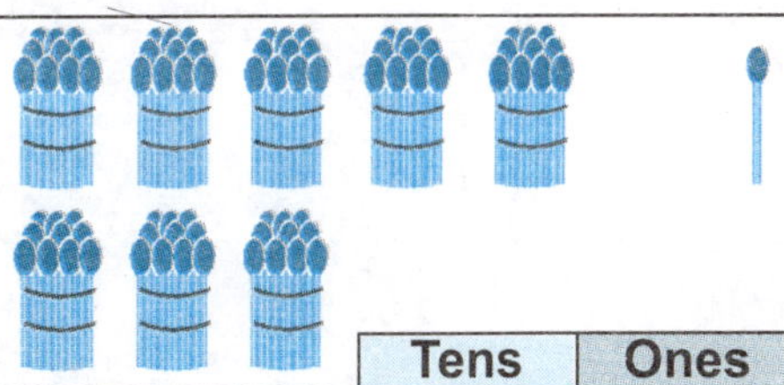

Tens	Ones

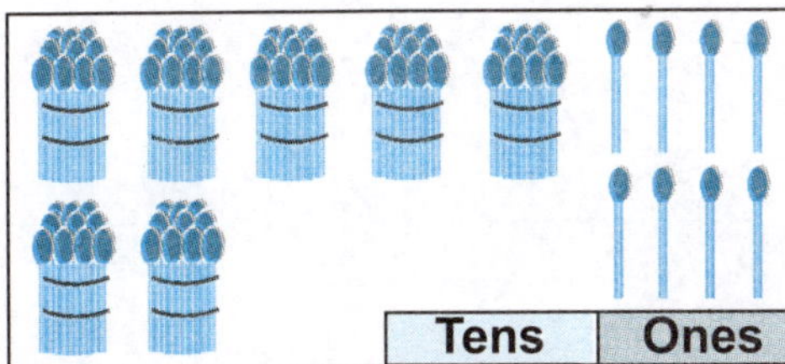

Tens	Ones

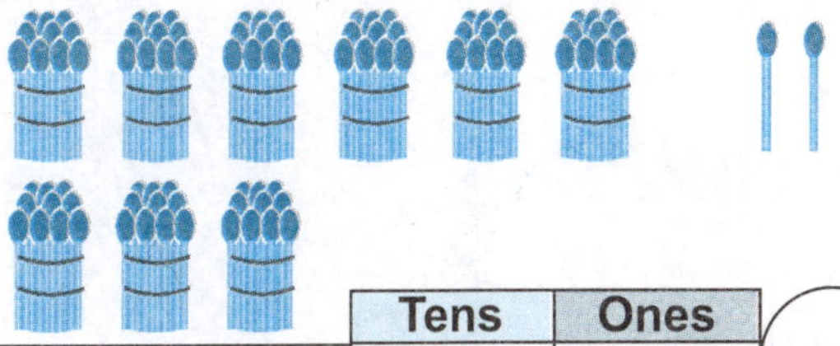

Tens	Ones

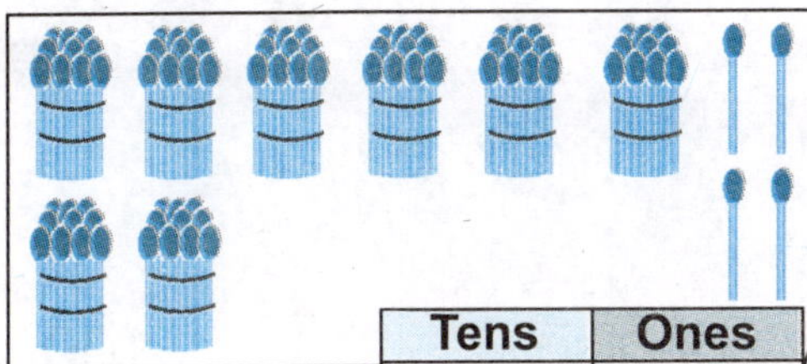

Tens	Ones

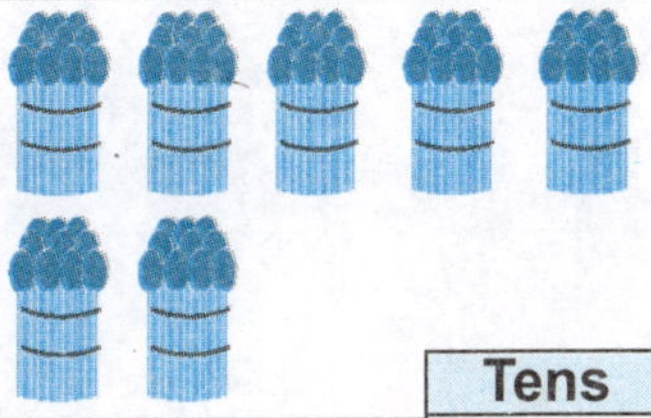

Tens	Ones

Teacher's Signature : ....   Date : ....

Assignment 38

Numbers

Complete the table :

1	2								10
		13							20
			24						30
				35					40
					46				50
51				55					
61			64						
71		73							
81	82								
91									100

Teacher's Signature : .... Date : ....

Test 9

A. Write the numbers :

1 ten 6 ones is ☐

2 tens 3 ones is ☐

3 tens 4 ones is ☐

4 tens 7 ones is ☐

5 tens 8 ones is ☐

8 tens 5 ones is ☐

B. Fill in the boxes :

8 tens ☐ ones = 83

5 tens ☐ one = 51

☐ tens 7 ones = 67

8 tens ☐ ones = 89

☐ tens 8 ones = 88

☐ tens 0 ones = 70

9 tens ☐ ones = 92

6 tens ☐ ones = 63

C. What comes just before and just after?

	45	
	83	
	38	

D. What comes in between?

79		81
23		25
66		68

Teacher's Signature : .... Date : ....

Assignment 39

Money

A. Tick (✓) the coins :

25 paise	
50 paise	
20 paise	
1 rupee	
10 paise	

B. Tick (✓) the notes :

2 rupees	
10 rupees	
100 rupees	
50 rupees	
20 rupees	

Teacher's Signature : .... Date : ....

Money

Assignment 40

Ring the correct amount of money :

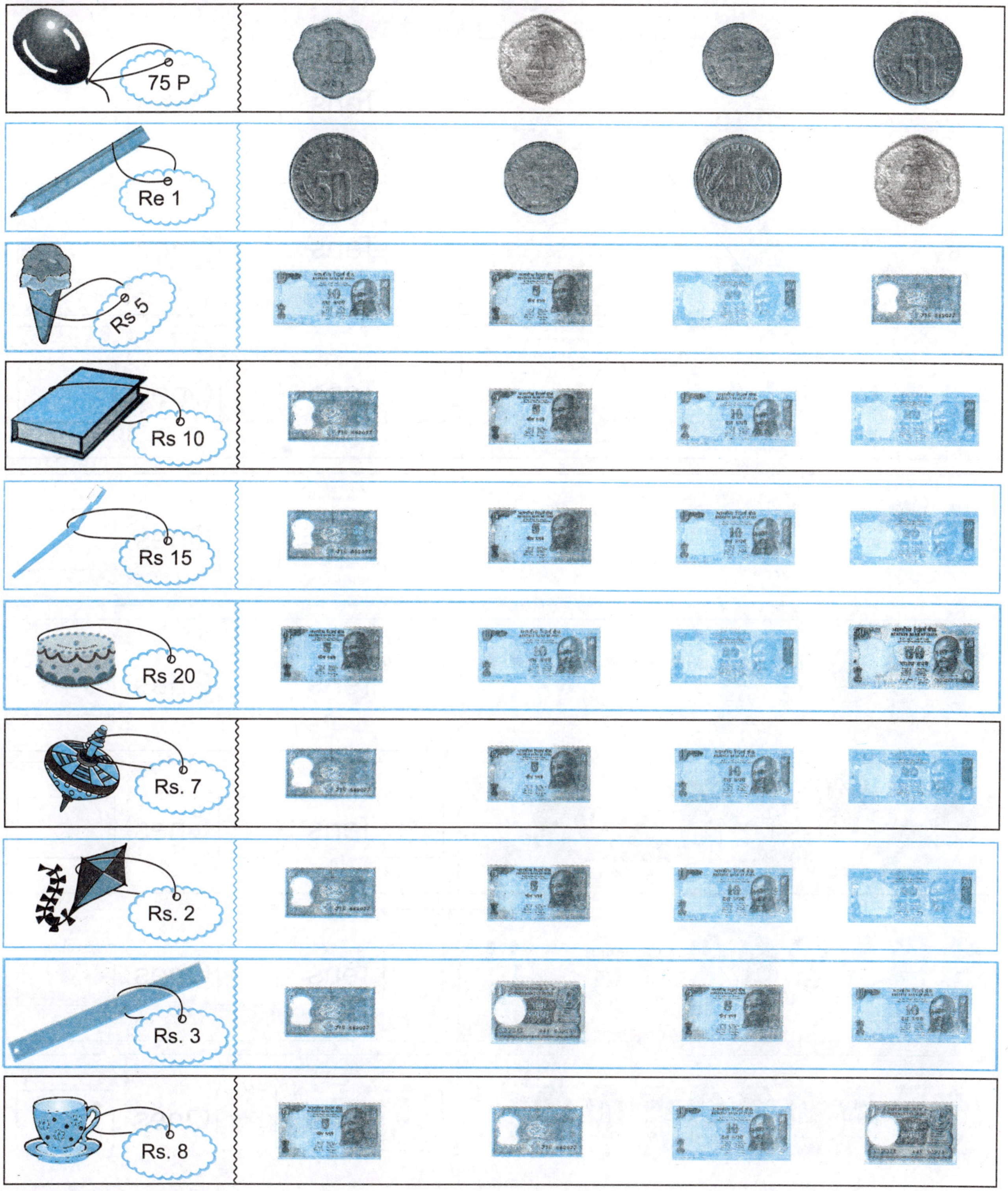

Teacher's Signature : ....

Date : ....

Assignment 41

How Many

Count and fill in the boxes :

Tens Ones

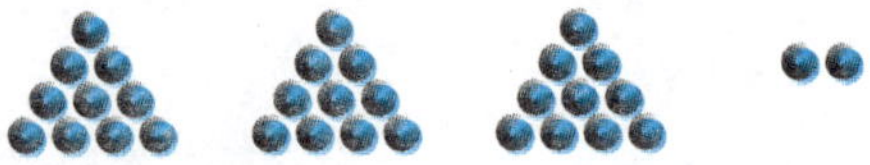

Tens Ones

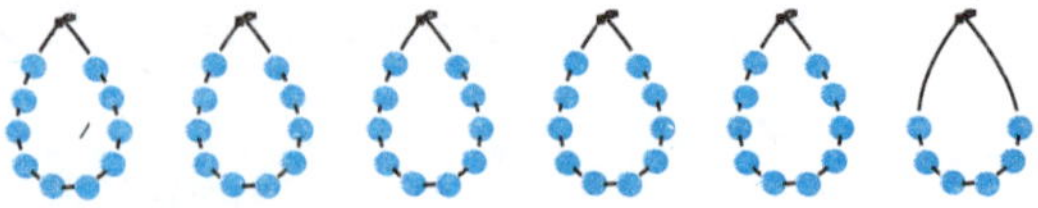

Tens Ones

Tens Ones

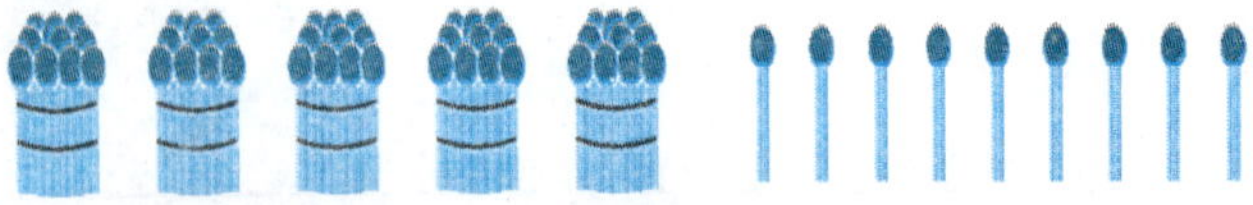

Tens Ones

Tens Ones

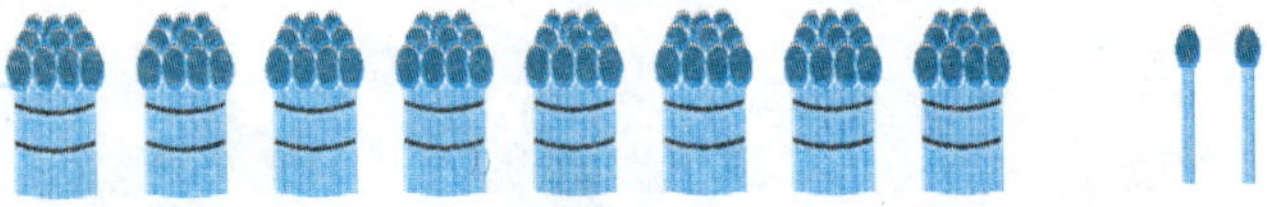

Tens Ones

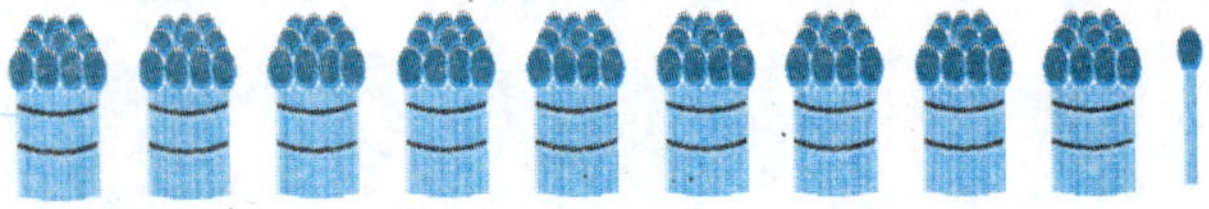

Tens Ones

Teacher's Signature : ....

Date : ....

How Many

Assignment 42

23 = ☐ Tens ☐ Ones

Write number name for 18. ____________________

Which is bigger : 26 or 62? ____________________

How many tens are there in 34? ____________________

5 tens and 6 ones is ____________________

2 taken away from 9 is ____________________

9 and 6 more make ____________________

20 is ☐ and ☐

5 parrots were sitting on a tree. 2 of them flew away. How many parrots are left on the tree? ☐

Mother bought 4 chocolates. Ravi ate all the four chocolates. How many chocolates are left? ☐

Teacher's Signature : ....

Date : ....

Test 10

A. Tick (✓) the note to buy the things :

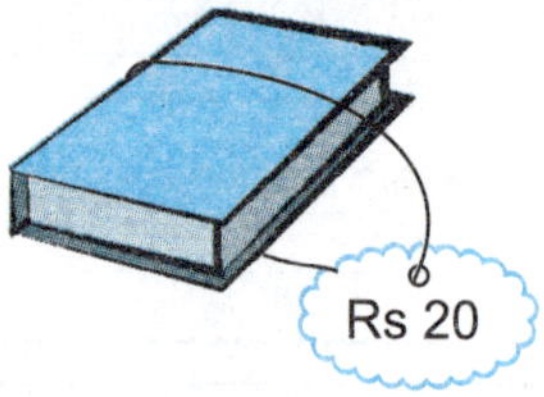	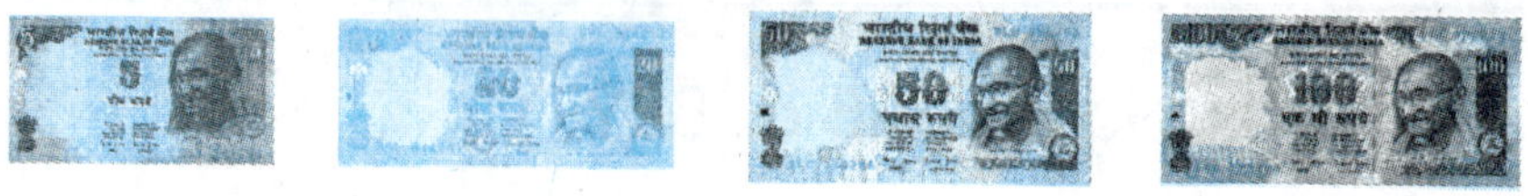

B. Tick (✓) the coin to buy the things :

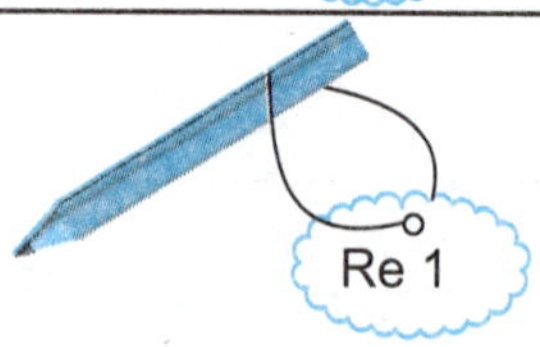	

C. Fill in the boxes.

The number just after 56 is ☐

How many ones are there in 10? ☐

53 is ☐ tens and ☐ ones.

How many tens are there in 70? ☐

If one banana costs Re 1, find the cost of 5 bananas. ☐

Teacher's Signature : .... Date : ....